ARTFUL BUSINESS

50 LESSONS FROM CREATIVE GENIUSES

Greg Stone

DEDICATION

All my love to my son Jack, Artist of Coding;
my daughter Lauren, Artist of Evolutionary Biology;
and my wife Mary, Artist of the Practical.

CONTENTS

Projecting Like an Artist

Mastering Applied Art

Eyeing the Mind, Minding the Eye

Mirroring Geniuses

Exploiting the Everyday

Venturing Where Only Artists Go

PREFACE: HOW THIS BOOK WILL HELP YOU

If you picked up this book, chances are you are a "thinking" businessperson, with some interest in the arts. Welcome.

You are about to discover that Michelangelo and a modern marketing executive, or Botticelli and a brand manager, have a lot in common.

If you want to learn how to describe a product or service in a more compelling way, how to reposition your company or how to find your muse, then this book is for you.

In each chapter you will see sumptuous art and stimulating ideas on facing pages, with probing questions to help you *see* in a way that will yield new perspectives on strategy or messaging.

You don't have to read this book from cover to cover. Instead, turn to any page at random for inspiration.

The 50 chapters are divided into six sections:

- *Projecting Like an Artist* (going beyond)
- *Mastering Applied Art* (learning the techniques)
- *Eyeing The Mind, Minding the Eye* (making visuals count)
- *Mirroring Geniuses* (thinking like the great ones)
- *Exploiting the Everyday* (using what's in front of you)
- *Venturing Where Only Artists Go* (traveling farther)

Please stay in touch. You can find me at gregstone.com.

ACKNOWLEDGMENTS

Without these museums, which generously shared images of the art in their collections, this book would not exist: The National Gallery of Art in Washington, DC, the Harvard Art Museums in Cambridge, MA and the Metropolitan Museum of Art in New York City.

Special gratitude to Danielle Carrabino, curator at the Harvard Art Museum, for invaluable insight into Caravaggio and the 17th century and for saving me from my ignorance; Isabella Donadio from the museum's image research department, for tireless assistance; and my friend Sree Sreenivasan, Chief Digital Officer at the Metropolitan, for ongoing support.

Many photographers were kind enough to share their work: the mysterious Pyanek; the supertalent Aaron Frutman; Michelangelo aficionado Dr. Jörg Bittner, who also enlightened me about the artist; wedding photographer Giuseppe Marano, who possesses the mind of Descartes; the superb Mark Ostow (who shot my photo and the portraits of Rebecca Lemov); Daniel Thomas Moran, poet, dentist and photographer, for the photos of his friend Samuel Menashe and for his thoughtful comments; Professor James Galbraith, who sent the photo of his father.

So many other creative people and organizations were forthcoming with their work and ideas: Nicole Bemboom and Gretchen Whittier of Arterra Landscape Architects in San Francisco; Pat Falco, artist of the deadpan; Jane Perkins, the Vermeer of discarded objects (a moniker I just gave her); Joseph Marioni, a charming and helpful man; Harvard Business School Professor Ryan Buell; Princeton Professor Adele Goldberg; my friend Susan Israel, political activist and artist; Kimberly Unger of the Denver Water Authority (whose ad seems to be missing something!); Mercedes-Benz; Qapital; Stacy Morris at BMW for *unprecedented* access to the archives of the company's *Art Cars* project; Clinton Piper at the Western Pennsylvania Conservancy (for the photo of *Fallingwater)*; and Dr. Pietra Kienle of Boehringer Ingelheim.

My good friend and former Time Inc. colleague Linda Gottfried, aka Den Mamma, designed the first cover and the basic page layout. Her work is exquisite, as always. See GraffitiWall.com for more details.

Editor/designer Jacob Eidsmoe created the current cover. Eternal gratitude to him for years of creative toil on my behalf.

Also thanks to Katie Ruland for the quick lesson on Adobe InDesign. Deep appreciation for Kristen Kusek, the first reader, and Sava Berhane, the second, who suggested dividing the chapters into separate sections. Both of these talented women were very helpful.

Thanks to Jim Franklin, copy (and content) editor extraordinaire, who gave me the benefit of his 43 years at *The Boston Globe*. My brothers from other mothers Greg Bauer and Phil Landa also had a hand in reviewing the manuscript.

Great gratitude to Gina Maccoby, my loyal literary agent, who taught me so much about the publishing world. She always speaks truth to her writers.

Special acknowledgments to Jim Grace, Robin Platt, Sree Sreenivasan (again), David Rollert and Harvard Business School Professor Dennis Yao for their kind words about the book. Dennis, I can't thank you enough for the detailed critique that made me probe deeper for relevant links to marketing.

To all of the Stone Communications clients: thanks for challenging me every day. You know who you are.

My mom and dad, Joan and Jack, gave me so much and made all things possible.

Again all my love to my beautiful and brilliant wife and children, Mary, Lauren and Jack, to whom this book is dedicated.

Any assets in this endeavor belong to those above; all mistakes are my own. I apologize if anyone is omitted.

PROJECTING LIKE AN ARTIST: INTRODUCTION

Critic Clive Bell used two words to summarize the appeal of art: significant form. You may be wondering what that has to do with you.

A personal story might help answer the question. I began my career as a writer at Time Inc. in New York, then moved halfway across the country to step in front of the camera as a TV reporter in Minneapolis. The most difficult part of an unfamiliar world of microphones, lights and cameras was recording narrations. Out of sympathy for my predicament, my boss sent me for voice lessons. The first thing the coach said was, "Remember, Greg, you have no charm."

I was dumbfounded. What did she mean? That I wasn't a nice guy? Not at all. Her point was that it takes more than warmth to hold an audience's attention. The best narrators are just a bit, well, arrogant. Their tone says, "If you don't listen, you'll be missing something."

Content alone won't carry a story. Significant form counts.

1: ART IS A TYRANT

Great art leaves you wanting more. It is an urgent and compelling experience, producing concentrated satisfaction. It creates a kind of superreality that is more stubbornly real than the everyday world, in a way that surpasses normal perceptions.

The process continues after, perhaps long after, you walk away from the museum, leave the theater or put down the book.

Art is news that stays new. Like a tyrant, it proclaims: "I insist that you stare at me. Turn away if you dare."

Look at Winslow Homer's *The Gulf Stream*. We can almost feel the wailing wind on our faces. We share the fisherman's fear as hungry sharks swirl round the tiny boat with the broken mast. Fortunately, a rescue ship looms on the horizon.

Yes, Homer puts us *right there*, in a way we just can't ignore.

Frank Lloyd Wright's masterpiece *Fallingwater* is equally compelling. On one level it is a home built over a waterfall, but it's much more than that. It's an inseparable combination of house and water — its own category — way beyond the realm of mere real estate.

 Does your message *demand* attention?

Winslow Homer, *The Gulf Stream*, 1899

Frank Lloyd Wright, *Fallingwater*, 1936 – 1939

2: NOTHING SUCCEEDS LIKE EXCESS

Exaggeration can certainly be effective, as 19th-century artist Honoré Daumier shows us. He is often called the Michelangelo of caricature.

Look at his lithograph of Victor Hugo. The writer is all head, and presumably all brain. Now compare that vision to the more realistic portrait by Alphonse Legros. We can see that Daumier's eye is quite accurate. The best parody has a strong basis in fact.

Yes, caricature fascinates. Neuroscientist V.S. Ramachandran and philosopher William Hirstein attributed the allure to the "peak shift" effect, that is, a vigorous response to exaggeration. Artists, they said, try to "capture the essence of something, but also to amplify it" into a "super stimulus."

We see exaggeration in successful marketing, too, often tinged with humor:

Altoids: "Mints so strong they come in a metal box."

Adidas: "Impossible is nothing."

 **Can you overstate your point *responsibly*?**

Honoré Daumier, *Victor Hugo*, 1849

Alphonse Legros, *Portrait of Victor Hugo*, 19th century

3: ARTIST VS. ARTIST

In the fifth century BCE, there lived a Greek artist named Zeuxis who drew first brush in a duel with his archrival Parrhasius to determine who could draw more accurately.

The haughty Zeuxis was certain of victory because the grapes in his work were so lifelike that doves actually tried to eat them. Yet when he asked attendants to remove the curtain covering Parrhasius's work, Zeuxis was dismayed to discover that the curtain *was* the painting.

Graciously conceding defeat, he said, "I fooled the birds, but Parrhasius fooled an *artist*."

 Is your content clever enough to make your *creative* teamstop and wonder?

Georg Hiltensperger, *Zeuxis in Front of His Painting of Grapes*, 19th century

ΠΑΡΑΣΙΟΣ

Georg Hiltensperger, *Parrhasius Fooling Zeuxis*, 19th century

4: EASY TO RECOGNIZE, HARD TO DEFINE

When I try to define art, the following list comes to mind:

A journey to the essence, a superior force, an affirmation, an action, a compression, a rearrangement of everyday items, a "we," a surprise, a metamorphosis, an evocation, a promise fulfilled, an answer to a question never asked, an antidote to the obvious — full of startling immediacy, bottomless connotations and keen insight.

In fact, and this is one of the central ideas in this book, this list could be applied to any transformational product, service or platform. Think of the PC, the iPhone, the internal combustion engine, penicillin and so on.

Just as painting is a triumph over nothingness, music over silence, film over darkness, sculpture over matter, so, too, is a great product a victory over an unmet need.

Back to the art world, here are two astonishing examples of creativity. For me, Tôkô Shinoda's *Screen with Abstract Designs* suggests quiet contemplation, with an undercurrent of apprehension due to the dark squares and spears or cracks that are intruding. No wonder that Shinoda, now 103, has been called the Japanese Picasso. She *forces* us to pay attention.

Going back a millennium, we see similar magnetism in a wall hanging made of macaw feathers from the Amazon jungles in eastern Peru. Textiles of this sort are said to be some of most sumptuous products of the so-called ancient world. The brilliant colors still delight today.

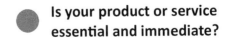 **Is your product or service essential and immediate?**

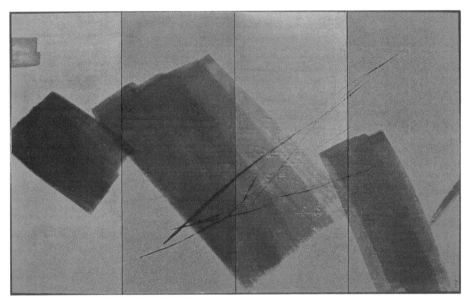

Tôkô Shinoda, *Screen with Abstract Designs*, c. 1974

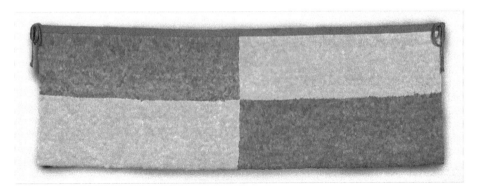

Feathered Hanging, Peru, 7th – 8th Century

MASTERING APPLIED ART: INTRODUCTION

Whenever I'm stuck, wondering how I'm ever going to generate an idea – any idea – I often pick up an art book and turn the pages. A quick glance at a Michelangelo, Pollock, Klee or Van Gogh, or for that matter a random walk through some poetry, can shock me out of my lethargy even when I think that it has all been done before and that there is no more room for innovation.

Too often we believe that we are starting with nothing. But there can be no such thing as "no thing." When I envision nothingness, I see an empty expanse of grayish space. Yet that is not even close to nothing, because 1) my mind conceived it, and therefore the *thought* is real and 2) there is an actual picture in my head.

That's probably what Wallace Stevens meant in his poem *The Snow Man* when he described "nothing that is not there and the nothing that is."

So when you *feel* as if you are starting from zero, the void is only apparent. Call up something, anything, relevant to the matter at hand.

If you truly have no ideas, then write down that you have no ideas. That alone is a starting point.

5: SEE THE "WE"

Spectators watch, imagine and participate. There is, after all, an artistic "we." Art expresses *us*, not just the artist, so we too are creators. As Edgar Degas said, "The artist does not draw what he sees, but what he must make others see."

In his painting *The Rehearsal*, doesn't it seem as if he's inviting us into the studio? An empty expanse of floor awaits our footsteps. We *belong* there.

Hierarchy disappears. Creator and audience join like two hemispheres of the same brain. The work paints us, the book reads us, the orchestra plays us.

Resonance means expressing what we feel but cannot say — uniting us with all others who experience a similar emotion. That's why we believe that our favorite musicians have written their songs about *our* lives.

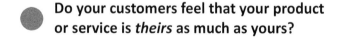 **Do your customers feel that your product or service is *theirs* as much as yours?**

Edgar Degas, *The Rehearsal*, c. 1873 – 1878

6: DECLARE WAR ON CLICHÉS

In many ways, art is the anti-cliché, running as far away from the commonplace as possible, turning the hackneyed on end.

Look at Leonardo da Vinci's drawing of the Madonna, who is ordinarily portrayed as a flawless icon. Here we see a disheveled and preoccupied woman, more accessibly human.

400 years later, Finnish painter Hugo Simberg surprises us in a similar way. We usually think of angels as guardians of the young, but here the reverse is true. Two boys carry a wounded angel with bloody wing and bandaged eyes. Her feet dangle lifelessly as she leans on locked elbows.

The boys look as somber as their clothes. One stares at us in defiant anger, as if to suggest that we are voyeurs, intruding on a sacred mission.

Oddly, the boys do not seem to be straining as they transport the angel. Perhaps she is so ethereal as to be weightless. Have we ever seen *anything* remotely like this before?

 Can you annihilate stereotypes?

Leonardo da Vinci, *The Head of the Virgin,* 1508 – 1512

Hugo Simberg, The Wounded Angel, 1903

7: TEXT AND CONTEXT

Look at the altered version of Vincent van Gogh's self-portrait, without the swirling background. Now compare the real painting below it.

In the original, the wild brush strokes, in concentric ovals around the artist's head, create an overpowering impression of instability, insanity and turmoil.

When the head stands alone, the stare is still laserlike, but the effect is less captivating.

Are you creating the best context, conceptually and physically?

Vincent van Gogh, *Self-Portrait,* 1889

8. FRAME IN, FRAME OUT

What do you include, and what do you "frame out?"

Our view of the world is limited by our peripheral vision, encompassing an arc of 135 degrees or so, but we have the luxury of choosing narrower boundaries for the images we create.

When I asked my go-to photographer Mark Ostow for his thoughts on this subject, he shared impressions of two versions of his portrait of Harvard Professor Rebecca Lemov:

> The wide shot provides a setting, giving the viewer additional information and context and making it clear that Rebecca is in a house. The tighter shot does not include much space around it. We don't know where she is or that she is looking through a window in a door. The focus is much more on her, not the environment. This changes the entire effect.

I count many frames within the wide shot: the edges of the photo itself, the border formed by the stairway post, the side of the door, and the sides of the window. The gentle sweep of the curtain (forming a sloping triangle to Rebecca's right) softens the hard lines and further focuses our attention on her face.

The closeup has fewer lines.

Which version do you prefer?

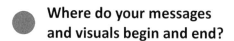 **Where do your messages and visuals begin and end?**

Mark Ostow, *Rebecca Lemov*, wide and tight photos, 2015

9: REACH YOUR OBJECTIVE (CORRELATIVE)

Famed poet T.S. Eliot said that the only way to evoke a particular emotional response in art is to establish a foundation in fact or circumstances. He called this the objective correlative, a fancy way of saying that you can't produce a feeling without the proper stimuli.

Edward Hopper understood this. His painting *Cape Cod Evening* creates the groundwork for an impression of quiet alienation. Each of the figures — man, woman and dog — is looking in a different direction, with no apparent communication. The long grass obscures their legs, the bottom of the house and the lower part of the trees, as if all are floating with no connection to the earth.

Now look at the spooky prominence of Mt. Katahdin in Maine in Marsden Hartley's painting. Even though the style is spare and the perspective nearly as flat as the canvas, we cannot help pausing to stare. The ludicrously symmetrical clouds and oversaturated red of the autumn leaves contrast with the dominant black silhouette of the peak.

Both of these paintings create an objective basis for feelings. T.S. Eliot would no doubt have called them successful.

Similarly, a targeted product or service may spark an emotional chord in the customer. But . . .

Have you laid the foundation for an emotional response from your customers?

Edward Hopper, *Cape Cod Evening*, 1939

Marsden Hartley, *Mt. Katahdin, Maine, No. 2*, 1939 – 1940

10. COLLABORATE WITH THE AUDIENCE

Tony Schwartz was a fiercely aggressive producer who made the infamous TV ad showing a little girl pulling petals off a daisy in support of Lyndon Johnson's presidential campaign back in 1964. The spot is very easy to find on YouTube today.

The girl counts uncertainly up to 10 and looks up in fear as a countdown to a nuclear explosion replaces her voice. A mushroom cloud fills the screen while Lyndon Johnson adds this narration: "These are the stakes. . . . We must either love each other, or we must die." The last line echoes W.H. Auden's anti-war poem *September 1, 1939.*

The ad aired just once, but that was enough to set the stage for Johnson's landslide victory over Senator Barry Goldwater, whom many regarded as a warmonger.

Schwartz's approach was closely allied with Eliot's, in that he believed that advertising should evoke, not provoke. He sought to elicit thoughts and feelings that were *already presen*t in the audience's mind rather than simply conveying inflammatory information. As Schwartz explained, "The listener's or viewer's brain is an indispensable component of the total communications system."

In other words, the audience completes the experience. Schwartz once said that people are born without earlids. "They listen to anything that concerns them."

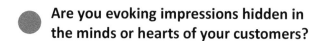 **Are you evoking impressions hidden in the minds or hearts of your customers?**

Tony Schwartz, stills from *Daisy Girl Ad*, 1964

11. WHAT *CAN'T* THEY SAY?

Like Schwartz's ad, art can be a conduit for emotions or impressions that we already possess. In some cases, though, a powerful image may spark feelings that we simply cannot describe.

For instance, Claude Monet's painting of fog on the Thames captures the bittersweet time in the morning when all things seem possible, but difficult to achieve. The sun is trying to shine, yet the water, sky, and fog have a blueish cast that seems to indicate . . . Well, you understand, even if words quickly fail.

That's why James Joyce called art the "speech of an emotion otherwise incommunicable."

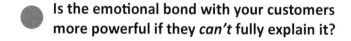 **Is the emotional bond with your customers more powerful if they *can't* fully explain it?**

Claude Monet, *Charing Cross Bridge: Fog on the Thames*, 1903

12. THE STYLE *IS* THE MATTER

The novelist Gustave Flaubert tortured himself in search of "le mot juste," the right word, and he would often spend a week on a *single* page.

For him, the language alone was so important that he dreamed of writing "a book about nothing . . . held aloft by the internal force of its style." He believed that the "most beautiful works are those that have the least matter."

Take a look at James McNeill Whistler's *Nocturne in Blue and Silver*. On one level, it depicts a blue harbor with smokestacks and a church spire in the background. Yet from another perspective, it might just be a study of the colors and their interplay. Is it merely its own subject, sort of an "immaculate perception?"

Similarly, Gustav Klimt's *Pear Tree* is about, well, a pear tree. Yet it's quite ornamental, almost like a tapestry. Each dot in the foliage represents a fruit, a leaf or a blossom. Do we see the collective impact of countless flecks of paint or the overall beauty of the tree? Does it matter?

Sometimes it's enough to offer a stylized image, without a lot of explanation. If you explain everything, you might ruin the glow and force of the idea.

 Is there a time when format or style may overpower content?

James McNeill Whistler, *Nocturne in Blue and Silver*,
c. 1871 – 1872

Gustav Klimt, *Pear Tree*, 1903 (reworked by the
artist 1903/1918)

13. IS MEANING OVERRATED?

When people see a work of art that is either abstract or puzzling, they'll ask, "What does it mean?" My friend Jon Sarkin, a gifted painter, answers with another question, "What does it mean to *you?*"

Then again, if you have to ask, you are either already intrigued, or perhaps already in trouble. "Everyone wants to understand art," Picasso said, but that's like trying to "understand the songs of a bird."

Henri Rousseau, whose talent Picasso instantly recognized, was largely a self-taught "primitive" artist who never left France. In this painting Rousseau shows us the banks of the Oise River, an unremarkable tributary of the Seine mainly used for commerce. Yet he turns the ordinary into a hallucination. The cows, disconnected from the trees behind, seem to float in the long grass even as they eat it. The flat perspective seems child-like.

So what does the painting mean? That Rousseau, who claimed he had "no teacher other than nature," discovered innocence there? Perhaps. Or maybe it shows that animals are oblivious to the complexities of life around them. Unseen barges may be floating by, full of consumer goods with no meaning to the cows.

Now look at Joan Snyder's *Summer Orange*. If we take her at her word, then we assume it depicts the pleasant colors of a season that runs from June to September in the Northern Hemisphere. Is that all, though? I see some menace in the paint literally bleeding down the canvas. Is Snyder's summer peaceful, turbulent or both? When you stare at the painting, can you find hidden messages?

Frank Stella said it best: "What you see is what you see."

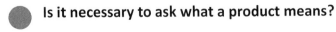 **Is it necessary to ask what a product means?**

Henri Rousseau, *The Banks of The Oise*, c. 1907

Joan Snyder, *Summer Orange,* 1970

14. LEAVE MORE UNSPOKEN

Look at the ad for Qapital, a savings app. It owes a clear debt to the abstractionists, especially Piet Mondrian, who managed to create the illusion of movement. The idea is that the app will help your chaotic finances coalesce into a viable plan. No words necessary.

Now look at the conservation ad for the Denver Water Department. I wonder how many people have sat down on the bench — either as a joke or because they weren't paying attention. The blank space certainly reinforces the idea that you should use only what you need.

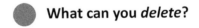 **What can you *delete*?**

Organize
your finances

www.qapital.se

Ad for Qapital

Ad for Denver Water Department

15. *PAINT* IT

Clients turned to Arterra Landscape Architects in San Francisco after water runoff damaged the foundation of their house.

Like painters, the designers began by doodling with colored pencils, as you see in the plan at the left. The solution? A sinuous swale, a sort of elegant storm drain, winding down the steep hill and blending seamlessly into the grassland. The end result is a garden with a warm palette — what they call a "hillside canvas" — with sweeps of fiery color discreetly escorting the swale.

Though the designer at Arterra said she had no particular artist in mind, I see Monet in the finished product.

What about you?

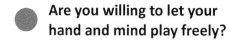 **Are you willing to let your hand and mind play freely?**

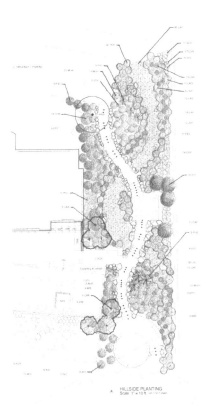

HILLSIDE PLANTING
Scale 1" = 10 ft.

Arterra Landscape Architects, *Plan for Swale*

Completed Project, Photo by Michele Lee Willson

16. DON'T ADD, MULTIPLY

In 1929, the Soviet director Lev Kuleshov produced a short film that revolutionized cinema. The movie first showed a closeup of a bowl of soup, followed by the face of an actor. The audience assumed he was hungry.

Then Kuleshov juxtaposed shots of a coffin and the actor. The assumption was that he was grieving. In a third scene, we see a reclining woman, then the actor. Conclusion: He was in love.

Yet in each case the actor's face was exactly the *same*. This is known as the Kuleshov effect.

The collision of the opposing shots was like multiplication, not addition. It was not A + B = C, but A X B = X, with the product X possessing a completely different meaning than either of the multipliers. Kuleshov's Russian countryman Sergei Eisenstein used this approach as the basis for a new editing technique that came to be called montage.

Philosophers call this dialectics: A clash between opposites (thesis vs. antithesis) yields a synthesis, and a new concept. Similarly, artists use contrasts between light and shadow, cold and warm colors, saturated and diluted colors and so on, to create unexpected impressions.

The same principle applies in writing: "My grave is like to be my wedding bed" (Shakespeare); "Float like a butterfly, sting like a bee" (Muhammed Ali); "April is the cruelest month, breeding lilacs out of the dead land" (T.S. Eliot).

 Can you combine contrasting ideas?

Still frames from *Lev Kuleshov film*, 1929

17. IT ONLY *LOOKS* EASY

If you study a Jackson Pollock painting and think, "That's easy, any child could do it," then I remind you that most blues songs consist of simple progressions. Just because you can play F, C and G chords on a guitar doesn't make you B.B. King or Robert Johnson, however. Simple doesn't mean easy.

I know. I tried my hand at painting in the style of Pollock. You can grade it yourself. For the briefest of moments I was proud of my endeavor. Then I showed it to a video editor I know who said it looks like something Pollock would have done in sixth grade. I have to agree.

You see Pollock wasn't just "Jack the Dripper." Filmmaker Stan Brakhage learned this when he visited the artist's studio. Though it was just morning, "Pollock had drunk most of a quart of whiskey," Brakhage said, and he was "like a lit stick of dynamite."

A group of critics were on the scene and one of them mentioned that chance played a role in Pollock's art. Whereupon Jackson rose to his feet, stuck a brush in a bucket of paint, swirled it around to remove the excess and hurled a gob of paint at a doorknob 50 feet away. Nailed it dead center.

"So much for chance," he muttered, "and that's the way out."

Are you brave enough to try something that might seem arbitrary at first?

Greg Stone, *In the Style of Pollock*, 2015

18. IS IT WORTH REPEATING?

Was Claude Monet in a rut? After all, he painted the pond behind his house in Giverny countless times: "It is not 200 meters around," he said, "yet its image awakens in you the idea of infinity."

When I visited the site with my family, I was struck by the modest size of the pond and the comparative magnitude of Monet's imagination. His keen eye scanned the scene like a camera, in closeups, wide shots and from many angles. Each painting is the same as all the others in many ways, but never boring.

Reiteration in messaging can be powerful, as long as there are distinguishing nuances or variations in emphasis.

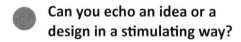 **Can you echo an idea or a design in a stimulating way?**

Claude Monet, *The Japanese Footbridge*, 1899

19. THE EYE AS A CAMERA

A camera can zoom in and out slowly, but our eyes jump from wide shot to tight shot in an instant. Try this: Lift your eyes from this page and look at the rest of the room where you are sitting right now. There will be no transition, just a sudden leap from small to larger vista. If you force yourself to notice the difference, however, the results can be dramatically insightful.

Let's take a look at Niagara Falls. Though many people think it is the highest in the world, it doesn't even rank in the top 500. At its zenith it is only 188 feet above the river.

In Sarah Wyman Whitman's closeup painting, the drama is exaggerated. But in the wide photo, the falls seem to shrink.

There is often a conflict between what you can see and what you cannot. That's why climbing to a balcony, literally or metaphorically, is a great way to gain perspective.

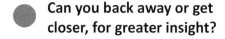 **Can you back away or get closer, for greater insight?**

Sarah Wyman Whitman, *Niagara Falls*, 1898

Saffron Blaze, *Niagara Falls photo*

20. IMPRESS WITH EXPRESSIONISM

Paul Klee called this watercolor *Southern Gardens*. Was the place really a collection of squares and rectangles? Of course not. But the gardens probably were bursting with yellow, teal and red flowers. The colors are realistic, even if the shapes are abstract.

The net effect is that the place is inviting and joyful. We want to *walk in*.

Artists like Klee were conveying what they *felt*, not just what they saw. That's the essence of expressionism, and the first two syllables, "ex-press," say it all.

Try to articulate your passion about your product or service and the emotions it might spark in the customer. Don't just *describe* the features; instead communicate a deep sense of enthusiasm, with colorful words.

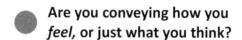 **Are you conveying how you *feel*, or just what you think?**

Paul Klee, *Southern Gardens*, 1919

21. MICHELANGELO TOOK IT AWAY

Michelangelo Buonarroti didn't choose just any old block of marble for his sculptures. He would spend weeks searching through the superb quarries at Carrara, which are still in use today. They're about 200 miles north of Rome (a great distance to travel in Michelangelo's time). He always sought the *perfect* stone that revealed to his acute eye the forms of the figures inside. For him, the marble actually *breathed*.

As a follower of Plato, Michelangelo believed that objects in the material world are mere examples of ideal forms that exist somewhere in divine space. He never thought he was imposing a design on the rock. Rather, he was simply extracting the form that was *already there* by chipping away the inessential, to reveal the inner Pietà.

You can employ this technique in managing people, by the way. Do not try to force your will on them. Don't draw, draw *out*.

If you look at Michelangelo's unfinished sculpture *Atlas*, you'll see the process at work. It's almost as if the form is struggling to escape.

Can you remove the surplus matter to reveal the vital?

Michelangelo Buonarroti, *La Pietà, 1498 – 1499*

Michelangelo Buonarroti, *The Atlas (or Bound)*, 1530 – 1534

EYEING THE MIND, MINDING THE EYE: INTRODUCTION

In your lifetime, you'll probably see 25 million different images.

If you're near trees or shrubs right now, look out your window. Now close your eyes. How many shades of green can you recall?

All told, the human eye can distinguish 10 million colors. This rich organ accounts for 75 percent of the information we receive. What's more, about half of our brain is dedicated to processing vision.

In a recent article, Professor Ryan Buell of Harvard Business School said, "Visual information is often privileged in perception and decision making." He and his coauthors Tami Kim and Chia-Jung Tsay cite evidence indicating that even static visuals affect our perceptions and tastes — starting early in life.

It is impossible to overestimate the importance of our eyes.

Hence the need for this section, and the book itself.

22. LOGOS, ARROWS AND BATONS

Did you ever notice the arrow inside the FedEx logo? Few people do, but it's there, perhaps as a subliminal message, conveying speed and precision. (Hint: it's between the E and the X.) Yet arrow or no arrow, the logo is instantly recognizable.

Now look closely at the London Symphony Orchestra logo. The initials L, S and O are there, though you may not see them at first. The image also suggests a conductor waving a baton. You have to look very closely. He or she could be facing toward us or away from us.

The vibrant images of ballerinas, a Degas trademark, are equally distinctive.

No one of these styles could be confused with any other.

 Do your images reflect your tastes, or your competitive advantage?

Edgar Degas, *Two Dancers Entering the Stage*,
c. 1877 – 1878

23. POWER TO THE PALETTE

What did Paul Gauguin mean when he said that color "is vibration [like] music" and that it can "attain what is most universal yet at the same time most elusive in nature: its inner force?"

Ia Orana Maria is one of his answers. It was his first significant canvas in Tahiti.

He described it this way:

> An angel with yellow wings reveals Mary and Jesus, both Tahitians, to two Tahitian women . . . Very somber, mountainous background and flowering trees . . . a dark violet path and an emerald green foreground, with bananas on the left. I'm rather happy with it.

Gauguin advised a young artist to make his colors *bold*:

> How do you see those trees? . . . If they are yellow, then make them yellow; and that bluish shadow, paint it with pure ultramarine; and those red leaves? Use vermilion.

 Is your business story vibrant enough?

Paul Gauguin, *Ia Orana Maria* (Hail Mary), 1891

24. MAKING MARBLE SWEAT

In her autobiography, St. Teresa describes an encounter with an angel in, well, starkly sexual terms:

> I saw in his hand a long spear of gold, and at the iron's point there seemed to be a little fire. He appeared to me to be thrusting it at times into my heart, and to pierce my very entrails. . . . The pain was so great that it made me moan; and yet so surpassing was the sweetness of this excessive pain, that I could not wish to be rid of it.

Gianlorenzo Bernini's sculpture *The Ecstasy of St. Theresa*, his favorite work, captures this supercharged moment. No wonder. He was a writer, producer and star actor who often staged scandalous exhibitions packed with sex and horror. In this sculpture his ribald imagination expresses itself fully, all in white marble. Here's how he described the challenge:

> If a man whitened his hair, beard, eyebrows, and — were it possible — his eyeballs and lips, and presented himself in this state to those very persons that see him every day, he would hardly be recognized by them. . . . Hence you can understand how difficult it is to make a portrait, which is all of one color, resemble the sitter.

Nonetheless, mere white marble can seem more colorful than a rainbow because of the isolation principle (put forth by Ramachandran and Hirstein). A single source of information can be less distracting and more expansive in its impact. That's why they suggest that more is less in art.

As Simon Schama wrote, Bernini could make marble fly, flutter, quiver and sweat, as if it were cinema in stone.

 Are you using color just for its own sake?

Gianlorenzo Bernini, *The Ecstasy of St. Theresa*, 1647 – 1652

The Ecstasy of St. Theresa, detail

25. SHADES OF TRUTH

Deep contrast between bright light and shadow is the essence of a style of painting called chiaroscuro, literally meaning "light/dark" in Italian.

Leonardo Da Vinci said "a luminous body will appear more brilliant" when surrounded by "deeper shadow." He even argued that shadow is more powerful than light.

We can see these principles at work in Michelangelo da Caravaggio's painting of St. Peter's denial of Jesus.

Note that the Roman soldier, barely visible in deep shadow, looks ominous as he points a dark, gloved finger signifying Peter's guilt by association. Meanwhile, a harsh white light falls on the eyes and headdress of the accusing woman and literally seems to lend clarity to her words.

Peter, on the other hand, is blanketed with a warm orange hue, midway between the light and dark rays around him, as if he is trapped somewhere between truth and lie.

The principle of chiaroscuro, broadly defined, has many applications: injecting silence into music (as Thelonius Monk often did); combining bitter and sweet flavorings (in the kitchen); commingling the vulgar and the sublime (Shakespeare); contrasting textures (smooth rock and sand) and so on.

 **Can counterpoint help?**

Michelangelo Merisi da Caravaggio, *The Denial of St. Peter*, c. 1610

MIRRORING GENIUSES: INTRODUCTION

This section is not about finding your inner genius or any such nonsense. Instead we'll work on emulating the *methods* of geniuses.

Ideas come to us at the most unexpected times. That's why I sliced a small Moleskine notebook into two smaller rectangles that easily fit into my back pocket — always ready to capture a thought. (Provided I remember to carry a pen, that is.)

I find that just looking at great art is itself stimulating. Or thinking about things that are scary or confusing. Or following Edgar Allen Poe's practice: Looking up three random words in the dictionary to spark new ideas. If that doesn't work, try three more; repeat as necessary.

Then again, you can start with this section.

26. START WITH MEDIOCRITY

If it is true that we know something only by its opposite, then we can understand art only by comparing it to the commonplace.

It's quite encouraging to look at the apprentice works of the great ones. Hint: The person who made this painting didn't start his career until he was 27. Here he's a long, long way from the heights he later achieved. This watercolor would probably get a middling grade in a beginning art course.

So, if you're stuck, write or draw the first things that come to mind. Random doodles are the raw materials of deeper thoughts. Don't try to be original at the outset. All talent begins in mediocrity.

See page 117 to discover the name of the artist.

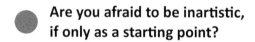 **Are you afraid to be inartistic, if only as a starting point?**

27. GO BACK TO GRADE SCHOOL

Paul Klee believed that children have innate artistic talent. He even said that some of his own early drawings were his most significant works.

Look at his watercolor *Little Hope*. Though Klee painted it at 59, it looks like the sort of casual abstraction that a child might create if you asked him what was on his mind.

If you get stuck, try to think like a grade-schooler. Or, better yet, try to remember what you would have thought as a child. You would have been much less inhibited then.

The poet Charles Baudelaire defined genius as "childhood clearly formulated" and regained at will. Bring it back.

 What would a seven-year-old say?

Paul Klee, *Little Hope*, 1938

28. HEAR THE COLORS, SMELL THE PICTURES

The composer Franz Liszt once told his musicians, "Gentlemen, a little bluer, if you please."

Like Liszt, those with synesthesia might associate letters or sounds with colors. In fact, I have a variant called spatial sequence synesthesia. As a consequence I envision numbers as a line with hash marks extending forwards and backwards in space. (I am happy to report that people with synesthesia are often creative.)

Even if you do not see the world in a skewed way, *try* to do so. Energy flows from one sense to another. If you can see music, hear colors or envision numbers in a different manner, you will gain greater insight.

Take Vassily Kandinsky. He believed that yellow represents high trumpet notes; blue, bass tones; green, violins; and red, strong drum beats. We can see hints of these transformations in *Improvisation 27,* subtitled *Garden of Love II*. If you look closely, you will also find images of couples embracing. No doubt there was music playing in the background.

 Are you engaging as *many* of your customers' senses as possible?

Vassily Kandinsky, *Improvisation 27 (Garden of Love II)*, 1912

29. SIGNS OF GENIUS

This may be a bit complicated, but ultimately very useful. Please bear with me.

The theory of signs, or semiotics, involves three elements: the signifier (the pointer, that is, the word or the picture); the signified (the concept); and the referent (the real-world object).

For example, the word "paint" (the signifier) consists of five letters on this page, indicating colored liquid (which is the signified idea), not to be confused with the real paint that an artist uses (the referent).

Look at Vincent van Gogh's *Wheat Field with Cypresses*. We see stalks tilting in the wind, clouds swirling every which way, mountains almost appearing to move and cypresses standing like ominous sentries over a sloping field. These objects are both referents and signifiers, pointing toward a signified impression of chaos, uncertainty, confusion and menace.

There are many signs at work, and signs of genius, at that.

 Does your product or service act as a *sign*?

Vincent van Gogh, *Wheat Field with Cypresses*, 1889

30. SIGNED AND DELIVERED

Sometimes the theory of signs requires, well, a sign. Take a look at Pat Falco's "sculpture," with a sardonic "label" that reads, "Cloud Installation, Abstract." Just in case you don't get it, an arrow points skyward.

Falco has been called the artist of the deadpan. As he told me: "I'm not the best at verbalizing my intentions, which I think is maybe why I started putting the signs in public in the first place. . . . Their purpose ranges from acting as a catalyst for conversation about city-related issues to bringing attention to underrecognized topics."

If Falco wanted to start a dialog, he certainly succeeded.

 **Can you add an actual sign to your communications?**

Pat Falco, photo from *Installation at deCordova Museum Biennial*, 2013

Falco closeup

31. METAPHORS OPEN DOORS

A metaphor is a particularly potent form of signage — an equation between dissimilars.

When Robert Frost wrote the "sun lets go ten million silver lizards out of snow" during a spring thaw, he was certainly not suggesting that reptiles actually emerged. He just meant that the rivulets were a sign pointing toward the concept of slithering lizards. This is semiotics in action.

Aristotle said that metaphors work best in two cases: when they convey information quickly (but not in an obvious way) or when they confuse us at first, as Frost's comparison may have done. If the images are puzzling initially, then the power of the sign lies in the conceptual distance from the referent. In other words, the harder we have to work to understand the comparison, the more satisfaction we derive.

Yet the strength of metaphors is not just conceptual. They can also engage our emotions, even unconsciously, according to new research by Professor Adele Goldberg of Princeton University. When participants in an experiment heard subtle metaphors like "She gave him a sweet compliment" as opposed to the more literal statement "She gave him a kind compliment," the part of their brains controlling emotions lit up during fMRIs.

In any case make sure that your metaphors (or analogies) don't go too far, otherwise they'll be like "feathers on the scales of a serpent," as philosopher Umberto Eco warned. On the other hand, if your imagery is too simple, it might seem condescending, as in "we're putting our arms around our clients."

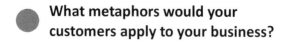 **What metaphors would your customers apply to your business?**

Lizards of Snow?

EXPLOITING THE EVERYDAY: INTRODUCTION

Most of the time you probably do not have the luxury of choosing your tools or vendors. Your boss asks you to shoot some pictures with your iPhone, instead of hiring a professional photographer. "Good enough is good enough," right?

There's an old saying often heard in newsrooms, where I spent many years at the beginning of my career: "Go with what you've got." If you're working on a tight deadline, you never have enough facts to write an eloquent 5,000-word magazine piece. Instead, you crank out a 500-word story and run with it.

Thinking outside the box? In an ideal world, yes, but we often have to work *inside* the box because we're limited by time, budget or resources. That's where the everyday comes into play. . . .

32. THE EXTRAORDINARY ORDINARY

Andy Warhol made a career out of recreating common items, like Campbell's soup cans, Brillo boxes and news photos, and legitimately calling them art.

This is nothing new. Giuseppe Arcimboldo used combinations of ordinary household objects to make portraits way back in the 1500s.

My favorite Arcimboldo is a portrait of a librarian, with head and body made of books, hair made of fanned-out pages and fingers of bookmarks. The materials make the man, literally. Shyly emerging from the darkness behind, pushing the curtain aside diffidently, he looks like a dusty book exposed to the light for the first time. His face is as inexpressive as the bland cover of an encyclopedia.

Now look at Jane Perkins' version of Jan Vermeer's *Girl with a Pearl Earring*. This is what this United Kingdom artist told me about her technique:

> I use any materials of the right size, shape or color: toys, shells, buttons, beads, jewelry, curtain hooks, springs, etc. No color is added — everything is used exactly 'as found'. The work needs to be viewed at two levels: from a distance to see the whole image and close up to identify the materials.

In many equally eloquent ways, the commonplace creeps into our language. Think of the metaphors we revere: "My cup runneth over"; "time is a thief"; the fog "comes in on little cat feet"; "there is no frigate like a book." Everyday images all.

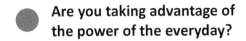 **Are you taking advantage of the power of the everyday?**

Giuseppe Arcimboldo, *The Librarian*, 1562

Jane Perkins, *Girl with a Pearl Earring, After Vermeer*, 2011

33. ART MARRIES THE ROUTINE

Yes, true communication often means finding the magical poetry in the commonplace. This concept is so essential that it merits this second chapter.

Look at the dramatic closeup of a grain of sugar shot by the Buenos Aires artist known as Pyanek. It looks like a crystal mountain.

Take a lesson from Giuseppe Marano — a wedding photographer from Florence — whose art far transcends the limitations of his profession. He told me he wants to depict a sort of temporary suspension of time, a weightless instant between one moment and the next, akin to a loss of consciousness. We see this mindset in the face of the preoccupied woman in shadow at the right of the photo of the garden scene.

Marano captured a similarly decisive moment in the life of a groom, seen from behind. His posture conveys security and gravitas as he looks forward, away from us, toward a new future with his bride.

Artists like Pyanek and Marano make finding the exotic in the everyday seem so simple. Unfortunately, this is very hard to do. Sometimes you just have to keep looking and looking. . . .

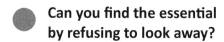 **Can you find the essential by refusing to look away?**

Pyanek, *Grain of White Sugar*

Giuseppe Marano, *Wedding Photo*

Giuseppe Marano, *The Groom*

34. AND THE REST OF THE MOVIE IS . . .

It has been my privilege to work on many video and photo shoots with Aaron Frutman, a brilliant photographer at home in all formats.

Like Norman Rockwell, Aaron can deliver an entire novel in one still frame: complete with heroes, plots and subplots.

Try to imagine the story behind each of these photos. Turn to page 117 for Aaron's explanations.

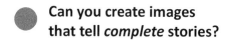 **Can you create images that tell *complete* stories?**

Aaron Frutman, *He . . .*

Aaron Frutman, *Wish You . . .*

35. A BRUSH WITH HISTORY

Virtually no one could surpass Anthony van Dyck in drawing the human face, especially his own.

The paintings here are not just self-portraits but complete, if condensed, *autobiographies.*

In the first work, at the top, I see a young man who is aristocratic, sly, mischievous and intelligent, with long, delicate fingers.

All this fits his bio: As the son of a wealthy cloth merchant from Antwerp, van Dyck spent much of his career abroad. He was fortunate enough to land a position for a time as a court painter in England for Charles I, who knighted him. Van Dyck liked to entertain lavishly and earned a reputation as a haughty and dissolute *artiste.* His life ended at 42.

The etching at the bottom, made a decade after the first work, shows his downslide in an instant. The body is blank (save for a faint outline) perhaps suggesting that he felt like an empty shell.

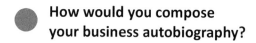 **How would you compose your business autobiography?**

Anthony van Dyck, *Self-Portrait*, 1620
– 1621

Anthony van Dyck, *Self-Portrait, From the
Iconography*, 1630

VENTURING WHERE ONLY ARTISTS GO: INTRODUCTION

Rules are overrated. Too often we imitate our elders or colleagues and call it success. Instead, we should learn from them, then go our own way. This is a simple concept that takes a lifetime to execute.

On the other hand, discipline does help. When I started my business some 25 years ago, I would often produce a dozen different concepts for a given project. Instead of dazzling clients, I confused them. And in their confusion, they would choose someone else.

Over time, I learned to present just three approaches, but I would make them as bold and original as possible.

If creativity doesn't come naturally, you might have to talk yourself into it. "Every morning when I awake, the greatest of joys is mine: that of being Salvador Dalí," the great artist said.

"Yeah," you're saying to yourself, "he was Dalí, and I'm not naturally creative."

No matter. Try to think in a divergent way. Focus on methods instead of goals.

36. BEAUTY ON THE SLANT

Most people think of beauty as symmetry, harmony, proportion or clarity. When we say that someone is attractive, we generally have the impression that his or her eyes, nose and mouth blend like a visual chord.

On the other hand, beauty is often found in the irregular, the unexpected, the surprising or the distorted.

Sandro Botticelli's *Virgin* is a case in point. At first, we see what appear to be perfect features. But look at the closeup. The face is uneven, the eyes are askew and the cleft in the chin points to her right.

The asymmetry and unusual geometry of the Virgin's features make her beauty even more dazzling.

**Are you brave enough
to make things lopsided?**

Sandro Botticelli, *The Virgin and Child*, c. 1490

Sandro Botticelli, closeup

37. WORD IS BOND

In marketing, positioning means owning *one word* in the customer's mind. When people think of FedEx, for instance, overnight comes to mind; for Dunkin' Donuts, awake; for Apple, elegance.

The same principle applies to writing. Here's Jorge Luis Borges, explaining how a word can be all encompassing in his short story *The Writing of the God*:

> What sort of sentence, I asked myself, would be constructed by an absolute mind? . . . [E]ven in the languages of humans there is no proposition that does not imply the entire universe; to say 'the jaguar' is to say all the jaguars that engendered it, the deer and turtles it has devoured, the grass that fed the deer, the earth that was mother to the grass, the sky that gave light to the earth.

Now look at Ellsworth's Kelly's untitled painting, showing red and blue curves. It is just that, a painting of red and blue curves, perhaps connoting sensuality, power or whatever else you happen to see. Yet at the same time it represents the essence of *all* such curves.

"The form of my painting is the content," he explained.

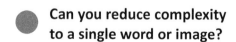 **Can you reduce complexity to a single word or image?**

Ellsworth Kelly, *Untitled*, c. 1964

38. EXPRESSION THROUGH COMPRESSION

The best messages are vital compressions, like bouillon cubes. The audience can simply add hot water and bring the soup to life. They'll be able to feel the steam on their faces, so to speak.

Samuel Menashe would have approved of this analogy. He was probably the best writer you've never heard of. Take a look at his poem *Dusk*. (Read it from the bottom up.)

Menashe's poems were as condensed as diamonds. "Minute cathedrals," in the words of critic P.N. Furbank. I spoke with Menashe's friend and fellow poet Daniel Thomas Moran, who described his method:

> Samuel wrote poems in his head and kept refining before he ever wrote them down. Sometimes it could take years. He called me once to announce that he had finally figured out what was wrong with a poem he had written in the 1950s. He removed the last line. The original was probably only six lines to start with.

The poet Rainer Maria Rilke would have endorsed this approach: "You ought to wait and gather sense and sweetness for a whole lifetime," he said, "and a long one if possible, and then, at the very end, you might perhaps be able to write 10 good lines."

Then there's Muhammad Ali. When he spoke at a graduation ceremony at Harvard many years ago a student shouted, "Give us a poem!" In an instant the champ said, "Me . . . we." Those two words, perhaps the shortest poem on record, gave voice to a deep concept.

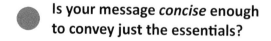 **Is your message *concise* enough to convey just the essentials?**

Dusk

night
into
earth
from
rise
Voices

Daniel Thomas Moran, *Samuel Menashe*, c. 2004

39. SIMPLICITY TAKES A LIFETIME

Artist Joseph Marioni told me, "It has taken me 45 years of professional life to master the form so it looks simple."

He fondly remembers the words of one of his professors: "Anyone can build a bridge with enough material. Success means building it with *just enough*."

Marioni illustrates that principle in his single-color paintings, which he believes are accessible and emotionally intimate.

Yet one color doesn't mean just one coat of paint. On the contrary, he applies as many as six layers and removes the excess with brushes, palette knives or even his hand. All this takes about four weeks, and it works only 70 percent of the time. (The rejects end up as carpet on his studio floor.)

For Marioni, the essence of painting is "unlanguaged," meaning that it can't be fully described in words.

Did you work hard enough to make the product simple?

Joseph Marioni, *Yellow Painting*, 1999

40. TAKE YOUR ART ON THE ROAD

Ah, the superhighway of art. BMW commissioned 17 artists, including Andy Warhol, Frank Stella, Roy Lichtenstein and David Hockney, to paint "art cars" as "engaging ambassadors for the brand."

Though the cars have been exhibited at the Louvre and the Guggenheim, the company insists that they are still, well, automobiles: "The 'second skin' of the painting does not dematerialize the car. . . . Despite all the artistry, the automobile is still present."

BMW says this is a spectacular experiment, at "the point where fascinating technology, design, cars and art intersect."

Andy Warhol painted his car in just 28 minutes, in an attempt to "give a vivid depiction of speed." As he said, "If a car is really fast, all contours and colors will become blurred."

Australian artist Ken Done wanted his "to look as if it was about . . . to fly, even if it was standing still." He certainly succeeded.

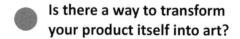 **Is there a way to transform your product itself into art?**

Andy Warhol, *BMW Art Car*, 1979

Ken Done, *BMW Art Car*, 1989

41. ACTION FIGURES

Philosopher Jean-Paul Sartre believed that words are another form of action — intended to shock the reader into awareness. In a similar vein, critic Harold Rosenberg coined the label "American Action Painters," apparently referring to artists like Jackson Pollock who "took to the white expanse of the canvas as Melville's Ishmael took to the sea."

Many creative people bring such aggression — is there any other word for it? — to their tasks. The body of the dancer in Rodin's sculpture thrusts forward like a knife. Even the toes on her back foot aim front, toward an imaginary goal.

Then comes *The Implorer*, by Rodin's lover Camille Claudel, who struggled with mental illness, possibly schizophrenia. The sculpture appears to embody her desperation, as the figure is literally reaching out for help.

Sometimes the kinetic energy is not quite so obvious. Mary Cassatt is often associated with fairly conventional portraits of women and children (so much so that she is sometimes called the painter of the nursery), but her conformist style concealed a strong will. Though her affluent family tried to dissuade her from a career in art, she was undeterred.

In this self-portrait we see this pioneering feminist's grim determination, reflected in her tense facial expression and squared shoulders. Her body and limbs are outlined in straight lines that further emphasize her decisiveness.

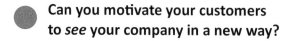 **Can you motivate your customers to *see* your company in a new way?**

Auguste Rodin, *Dance Movement I*, 1911

Camille Claudel, *The Implorer*, 1898 and c. 1905

Mary Cassatt, *Portrait of the Artist*, 1878

42. YOU CAN'T ALWAYS HANG IT ON THE WALL

Conceptual art may seem bizarre at first impression. In 1969, Vito Acconci had himself photographed as he followed random people on the streets of New York. A few years later, artist Fred Forest published blank space in a French newspaper where readers could draw their own pictures. More recently, Christo and his wife Jeanne-Claude placed 7,500 fabric gates on paths in Central Park in New York City.

These "conceptual" artists create events, not just objects.

Yet this is no longer a sideshow. In fact, it is nearly mainstream. In 2009, the curator of media at the Museum of Modern Art in New York City expanded his title to include performance art. Soon afterwards, Marina Abramovic engaged in staring contests with all comers there in a work called *The Artist is Present*. All told, she sat motionless in a chair six days a week for a total of 700 hours under bright lights in a huge atrium.

Abramovic is now a major "brand," with photos of her performances fetching as much as $365,000.

On the political front, architect and social entrepreneur Susan Israel uses public art to focus attention on climate change in installations like *Rising Tides*. The colored fish at a transit station in Boston show three levels of storm surges: high tide now, in 2050 and in 2100.

"People were stunned," Israel says. "It was the first time they understood what rising seas meant for them personally. We make the unseen visible and hear 'Wow' at every installation."

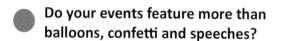 **Do your events feature more than balloons, confetti and speeches?**

Christo & Jeanne-Claude, *The Gates*, 2005

Susan Israel, *Rising Tides*, public art at Courthouse T Station in Boston, 2014

43. PLAY IT AS IT LIES

If we define a lie either as an intentionally false statement or a form of deception, then can we say that all art is false? Perhaps, if we regard a painting as a deliberate amplification or distortion of reality, or an attempt to "mislead" the viewer by showing her only what we want her to see.

In this context, we're in great company. Pablo Picasso once said, "Art is a lie that enables us to realize the truth."

Then comes Stefani Joanne Angelina Germanotta, better known by another name. She says, "People say Lady Gaga is a lie and they are right. I am a lie. And every day I kill to make it true."

In my "painting" you can see that misstatements can be disorienting, but they also make us see the commonplace in a skewed way.

Please understand that I am not in any way suggesting that businesses should distort the truth. I am saying, however, that a little ambiguity might go far.

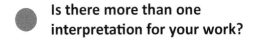 **Is there more than one interpretation for your work?**

BLUE YELLOW GREEN **WHITE**

BLACK BROWN GREEN ORANGE

WHITE RED YELLOW PURPLE

TEAL CRIMSON **PINK** WHITE

Greg Stone, *True Colors*, 2015

44. PRACTICAL GRAMMAR

Please bear with me. Predicates have deep relevance for communications. So what is a predicate? A descriptor linked with the subject of a sentence to provide additional information.

A predicate can be a verb, as in "Vincent paints," with the act of painting defining Vincent. A predicate can also be a noun (painter) or an adjective (talented), as in "Vincent was a painter" or "He was talented."

Just as the media extend our senses, as famed theorist Marshall McLuhan argued, so too can transformative products that are bundles of physical and psychological attributes intensify our lives as *predicates*. As Charles Revson famously quipped, "In the factory, we make cosmetics; in the drugstore, we sell hope." It's no longer verb-direct object ("I want perfume"); it's now subject-predicate ("I am the hope I am purchasing.")

Products thus can *reflect and even embody* our desires and our very identities by imposing new concepts on the norms of everyday life.

Look at the Mercedes-Benz *Blind Spot Assist ad*, touting a radar sensor that monitors the area around your car and warns you if another vehicle is alongside. The system can even apply the brakes if you try to turn at a dangerous moment.

The ad shows how the technology transforms the driver into a cubist vision, mimicking the action of the radar. Thes copy completes the picture: "Side view, without turning around."

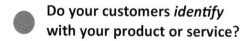 **Do your customers *identify* with your product or service?**

Mercedes-Benz, *Blind Spot Assist Ad*

45. ART IN THE LAB, SCIENCE ON THE EASEL

Most people think that scientists and artists have nothing in common, but there is growing evidence that the creative process in both fields is similar.

It is a common misconception that scientists first collect facts, then derive a hypothesis (by the process of *induction*). The late P.B. Medawar, a Nobel-Prize winning biologist, said the opposite is true. The idea often comes first, then the testing, in a *deductive* way.

Artists use a similar approach: the concept precedes the execution and validation.

Inventors in business often function this way too. There is no doubt, for instance, that Steve Jobs' mind worked deductively, and perhaps that's why he was so skeptical about market research. "Customers don't know what they want until you show it to them," he said. "Our task is to read things that are not yet on the page."

Like Jobs, artists are sometimes so intuitive that they discover scientific concepts on their own. For instance, Vincent van Gogh seemed to instinctively understand the phenomenon of turbulence in fluid dynamics, which some experts say is harder to fathom than quantum mechanics. For instance, the patterns in the clouds in *Green Wheat Fields* mimic whirlpools cascading into smaller and smaller circles.

You see, science and art are not just cousins. They're siblings.

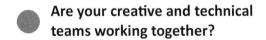 **Are your creative and technical teams working together?**

Vincent van Gogh, *Green Wheat Fields, Auvers*, 1890

46. PARADOX IS ORTHODOX

If you want to be a more creative manager, you need to be comfortable with paradoxes, that is, apparent contradictions. Pursuing inconsistent goals is an integral part of a leader's job, in that she or he must simultaneously manage the present and innovate for the future.

Paradoxes certainly creep into marketing. Starburst, for instance, produced an ad with this tagline: "Tropical but thoroughly enjoyed by pale people who burn easily. It's a pack of contradictions."

Another example is HSBC's slogan: "The world's local bank."

Now look at the ad for the pain reliever Thomapyrin, from Boehringer Ingelheim: "The barber of Seville shaves all men of Seville, except the ones who shave themselves." So who shaves him?

Needless to say, the puzzle can give you a headache, which is the joke. But how do you resolve the dilemma? If the barber shaves all those who don't shave themselves and not the ones who do, then he is breaking the rule if he shaves his own face. There is no logical solution, unless you assume that all men in town, including the barber, are un-shaven. If they all shave, however, then such a place could not exist.

Sometimes you just have to let the confusion stand.

 Can unresolved contradictions work?

Thomapyrin Paradox ad

47. INSPIRATION AT 80 PROOF

Some of our greatest writers had outsized appetites for drink or drugs.

O. Henry, Dylan Thomas, Dorothy Parker, Edgar Allen Poe, Jack Kerouac, William Faulkner, Ernest Hemingway, James Joyce, F. Scott Fitzgerald — all were said to be alcoholics. Samuel Coleridge, Elizabeth Barrett Browning, Charles Baudelaire, Jean-Paul Sartre — drug users.

Now comes research showing that a bit of alcohol may actually spur creativity. A study in the rather sober-sounding academic journal *Consciousness and Cognition* shows that men who drank moderate amounts of vodka and cranberry juice not only performed better and faster on word association tests but were also more likely to feel a sudden rush of insight.

Could it be that alcohol, by reducing inhibitions, allows the mind to play more freely and to see hidden connections more readily?

Please understand that I am not advocating drinking. I am merely suggesting that an occasional drink may prevent a logjam. Hemingway would certainly not disagree.

 Is there a way to disinhibit your mind?

Robert Capa, *Ernest Hemingway during a shooting party*, 1940 – 1941

48. MAKING SENSE IS SO 20TH CENTURY

You may have heard of postmodernism (po-mo), a form of art featuring a hodgepodge of styles and genres, with no linear narrative, often with an ironic, mischievous edge. There may be a story with a beginning, middle and end, though not necessarily in that order.

In architecture, we have a type of po-mo called deconstructivism, characterized by distortion and controlled anarchy.

Case in point: *The Dancing House* in Prague, designed by Frank Gehry and Vlado Milunić. The winding moldings, off-kilter windows and leaning towers create an impression that the building is trying to leap off the ground.

No wonder that Gehry originally called the project *Fred and Ginger*, after Fred Astaire and Ginger Rogers, as it literally personifies the two Hollywood stars. The "Fred" tower, on your right, is a concrete cylinder standing straight and tall. The slimmer "Ginger" wears a glass dress. She seems to be dancing away on graceful legs in the form of pillars.

As Milunić said, the building is "bursting at its seams" and is "charged with internal energy."

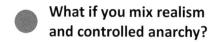 **What if you mix realism and controlled anarchy?**

Frank Gehry and Vlado Milunić, *Dancing House*, 1992 – 1996

49. COLLECT THE EFFECT

Is it true that art = a concept made concrete?

Beethoven reportedly said, "I turn my ideas into tones which resound, roar and rage until at last they stand before me [as] notes."

In a similar process, the painter Odilon Redon seemed to delight in transforming his thoughts, dreams or hallucinations into tangible form. In this pastel, called simply *Head of a Young Women*, a mysterious animal slithers down the wall, an orb hovers in front and a yellow halo surrounds the subject's head.

The captivating colors enhance the hypnotic effect. It is at once a portrait of a specific young woman and a general statement about reverie. Her gaze is unforgettable.

 Are you releasing the *full impact* of your work?

Odilon Redon, *Head of a Young Woman*, 19th – 20th century

50. WAITING FOR YOUR MUSE IS NO EXCUSE

So where do you go from here?

Take a lesson from Pablo Picasso and famous economist John Kenneth Galbraith. What could they possibly have in common?

Picasso said, "Inspiration does exist, but it must find you working."

So where does John Kenneth Galbraith fit in? In my prior life as a journalist, I interviewed him many times. He was not only uncommonly tall at six foot eight, but uncommonly prolific as well, even writing a novel in his 80s and economics books well into his 90s. He called writing a "bad habit" that consumed several hours each morning.

Yet he scoffed at the concept of inspiration. "That spontaneous quality that critics so admire in my prose," he told me, "usually comes on the fourth or fifth draft."

If you wait for ideas, they may never come.

 Put down this book and get after it.

Rene Burri, *Pablo Picasso*, 1957

John Kenneth Galbraith, c. 1996

ANSWERS TO QUESTIONS

From pages 63 and 64:

This is an early van Gogh, from 1879. It is called *Coke Factory in the Borinage.*

From pages 81 and 82:

Here is Aaron Frutman's story about the basket weaver, whose photo is called *He Made this in an Hour:*

> In a small town called San Juan de Oriente in Nicaragua, I cut through an alley in a rush to get to the next shot down the street. I ran into this gentleman who was totally immersed in his work. He was moving so quickly that I'd bet he could crank out two or three of these baskets a day. The man was clearly an artist and never once looked up while I photographed him.

And now Aaron's story about the musician, whose picture is called *Wish You Could Hear his Tunes*:

> He was playing the instrument on the bridge in Mostar, Bosnia. He survived a war and now scrapes together a living from tips from the tourists crossing the bridge. He could carry a tune, but there was a sadness in his voice that conveyed a sense of emptiness. He looks probably 15 years older than he really is.

You can almost *hear* the music, can't you?

PICTURE CREDITS

Cover, Johannes Vermeer, *Girl with a Pearl Earrning*, c. 1665, photo by Ian Dagnall/Alamy Stock Photo (headshot only).

Cover, Michelangelo Buonarroti, *David*, 1501 – 1504, photo by Gilmanshin/Shutterstock, Inc. (headshot only).

P. 8, Winslow Homer, *The Gulf Stream*, 1899, courtesy of the Metropolitan Museum of Art, New York, NY, Catharine Lorillard Wolfe Collection, Wolfe Fund, 1906.

P. 8, Frank Lloyd Wright, *Fallingwater*, 1936 – 1939, photo courtesy of the Western Pennsylvania Conservancy.

P. 10, Honoré Daumier, *Victor Hugo*, 1849, courtesy of the Metropolitan Museum of Art, New York, NY, gift of Harry G. Friedman, 1954, Accession Number: 54.557.7.

P. 10, Alphonse Legros, *Portrait of Victor Hugo*, 19th century, courtesy of Harvard Art Museums/Fogg Museum, Cambridge, MA, bequest of Grenville L. Winthrop, 1943.865, photo: Imaging Department © President and Fellows of Harvard College.

P. 12, Georg Hiltensperger, *Zeuxis in Front of his Painting of Grapes*, 19th century, courtesy of the State Hermitage Museum, St. Petersburg, Russia, photograph © the State Hermitage Museum, by T.V. Gorbokoneva.

P. 12, Georg Hiltensperger, *Parrhasius Fooling Zeuxis*, 19th century, courtesy of the State Hermitage Museum, St. Petersburg, Russia, photo © The State Hermitage Museum, by T.V. Gorbokoneva.

P.14, Tôkô Shinoda, *Screen with Abstract Designs*, c. 1974, courtesy of Harvard Art Museums/Arthur M. Sackler Museum, Cambridge, MA, gift of Jose M. and Liliane Soriano, 1997.121, photo: Imaging Department © President and Fellows of Harvard College.

P. 14, *Feathered Hanging*, Peruvian, 7th – 8th Century, courtesy of the Metroplitan Museum of Art, New York, NY, The Michael C. Rockefeller Memorial Collection, bequest of Nelson A. Rockefeller, 1979, Accession Number: 1979.206.467.

P. 18, Edgar Degas, *The Rehearsal*, c. 1873 – 1878, courtesy of Harvard Art Museums/Fogg Museum, Cambridge, MA, bequest from the Collection of Maurice Wertheim, Class of 1906, 1951.47, photo: Imaging Department © President and Fellows of Harvard College.

P. 20, Leonardo da Vinci, *The Head of the Virgin*, 1508 – 1512, courtesy of the Metropolitan Museum of Art, New York, NY, Harris Brisbane Dick Fund, 1951, Accession Number: 51.90.

P. 20, Hugo Simberg, The Wounded Angel, 1903, courtesy of Ateneum Art Museum, Ahlström collection, photo: Finnish National Gallery/Hannu Aaltonen.

P. 22, Vincent van Gogh, *Self-Portrait*, 1889, courtesy of The National Gallery of Art, Washington, D.C., Collection of Mr. and Mrs. John Hay Whitney, Accession Number: 1998.74.5.

P. 24, Mark Ostow, *Portraits of Rebecca Lemov*, 2015, courtesy of the photographer and the subject.

P. 26, Edward Hopper, *Cape Cod Evening*, 1939, courtesy of The National Gallery of Art, Washington, D.C., John Hay Whitney Collection, 1982.76.6.

P. 26, Marsden Hartley, *Mt. Katahdin, Maine, No. 2*, 1939 – 1940, courtesy of The Metropolitan Museum of Art, New York, NY, Edith and Milton Lowenthal Collection, bequest of Edith Abrahamson Lowenthal, 1991, Accession Number: 1992.24.3.

P. 28, Tony Schwartz, stills from *Daisy Girl Ad*, 1964.

P. 30, Claude Monet, *Charing Cross Bridge: Fog on the Thames*, 1903, courtesy of Harvard Art Museums/Fogg Museum, Cambridge, MA, gift of Mrs. Henry Lyman, 1979.329, photo: Imaging Department © President and Fellows of Harvard College.

P. 32, James McNeill Whistler, *Nocturne in Blue and Silver*, c. 1871 – 1872, courtesy of Harvard Art Museums/Fogg Museum, Cambridge, MA, bequest of Grenville L. Winthrop, 1943.176, photo: Imaging Department © President and Fellows of Harvard College.

P. 32, Gustav Klimt, *Pear Tree*, 1903 (reworked by the artist 1903/1918), courtesy of Harvard Art Museums/Busch-Reisinger Museum, gift of Otto Kallir, BR66.4, photo: Imaging Department © President and Fellows of Harvard College.

P. 34, Henri Rousseau, *The Banks of the Oise*, c. 1907, courtesy of Harvard Art Museums/Fogg Museum, Harvard Art Museums/Fogg Museum, Cambridge, MA, bequest from the Collection of Maurice Wertheim, Class of 1906, 1951.67, photo: Imaging Department © President and Fellows of Harvard College.

P. 34, Joan Snyder, *Summer Orange*, 1970, courtesy of Harvard Art Museums/Fogg Museum, Cambridge, MA, gift of Michael Walls (GSD, Class of 1961-1963) in memory of his parents, John Alvin James Williamson Walls and Elva Mary Claire Ricciardi Walls, 2007.225, photo: Imaging Department © President and Fellows of Harvard College

P. 36, *Organize Your Finances Ad*, courtesy of Qapital, Perniclas Bedow, designer.

P. 36, *Use Only What You Need Ad,* courtesy of Denver Water Department.

P. 38, Sketch and photo courtesy of Arterra Landscape Architects, San Francisco, CA, photo by Michele Lee Willson.

P. 40, Stills from *Lev Kuleshov film*, 1929.

P. 42, Greg Stone, *In the Style of Pollock*, 2015.

P. 44, Claude Monet, *The Japanese Footbridge*, courtesy of the National Gallery of Art, Washington, D.C., gift of Victoria Nebeker Coberly, in memory of her son John W. Mudd, and Walter H. and Leonore Annenberg, Accession Number: 1992.9.1.

P. 46, Sarah Wyman Whitman, *Niagara Falls*, 1898, courtesy of Harvard Art Museums/Fogg Museum, Harvard Art Museums/Fogg Museum, gift of Mary C. Wheelwright, 1939.251, photo: Imaging Department © President and Fellows of Harvard College.

P. 46, Saffron Blaze, *Niagara Falls*.

P. 48, Paul Klee, *Southern Gardens*, 1919, courtesy of The Metropolitan Museum of Art, New York, NY, The Berggruen Klee Collection, 1984, Accession Number: 1984.208.2.

P. 50, Michelangelo Buonarroti, *La Pietà*, 1498 – 1499, photo by pandapaw, Shutterstock, Inc.; *The Atlas (or Bound)*, 1530 – 1534, photo by Dr. Jörg Bittner.

P. 54, Federal Express and London Symphony Orchestra logos.

P. 54, Edgar Degas, *Two Dancers Entering the Stage*, c. 1877 – 1878, courtesy of Harvard Art Museums/Fogg Museum, Cambridge, MA, bequest of Grenville L. Winthrop, 1943.812, photo: Imaging Department © President and Fellows of Harvard College

P. 56, Paul Gauguin, *Ia Orana Maria* (Hail Mary), 1891, courtesy of The Metropolitan Museum of Art, New York, NY, bequest of Sam A. Lewisohn, 1951, Accession Number: 51.112.2.

P. 58, Gianlorenzo Bernini, *The Ecstasy of St. Theresa*, 1647 – 1652, photo by Dnalor 01, tight shot photo by Nina Aldin Thune.

P. 60, Michelangelo Merisi da Caravaggio, *The Denial of St. Peter*, c. 1610, courtesy of the Metropolitan Museum of Art, New York, NY, gift of Herman and Lila Shickman, and purchase, Lila Acheson Wallace Gift, 1997, Accession Number: 1997.167.

P. 64, Vincent Van Gogh, *Coke Factory in the Borinage*, 1879, courtesy of Van Gogh Museum, Amsterdam (Vincent van Gogh Foundation), Accession Number: d370V1962, F1040.

P. 66, Paul Klee, *Little Hope*, 1938, courtesy of the Metropolitan Museum of Art, New York, NY, The Berggruen Klee Collection, 1984, Accession Number: 1984.315.58.

P. 68, Vassily Kandinsky, *Improvisation 27 (Garden of Love II)*, 1912, courtesy of the Metropolitan Museum of Art, New York, NY, Alfred Stieglitz Collection, 1949, Accession Number: 49.70.1.

P. 70, Vincent Van Gogh, *Wheat Field with Cypresses*, 1889, courtesy of the Metropolitan Museum of Art, New York, NY, purchase, The Annenberg Foundation Gift, 1993, Accession Number: 1993.132.

P. 72, Pat Falco, photo from *Installation at the deCordova Museum Biennial*, Lexington, MA, 2013, courtesy of the artist.

P. 74, *Lizards of Snow?*, photo by chinahbzyg, Shutterstock, Inc.,

P. 78, Giuseppe Arcimboldo, *The Librarian*, 1562, courtesy of the Skokloster Castle Museum, Håbo Municipality, Sweden.

P. 78, Jane Perkins, *Girl with a Pearl Earring, After Vermeer*, 2011, courtesy of the artist.

P. 80, Pyanek, *Grain of White Sugar*, courtesy of the photographer/artist.

P. 80, Giuseppe Marano, *Wedding Photos,* courtesy of the photographer.

P. 82, Aaron Frutman, *He Made This in an Hour* and *Wish You Could Hear His Tunes,* courtesty of the photographer.

P. 84, Anthony van Dyck, *Self-Portrait*, 1620 – 1621, courtesy of the Metropolitan Museum of Art, New York, NY, The Jules Bache Collection, 1949, Accession Number: 49.7.25.

P. 84, Anthony Van Dyck, *Self-Portrait, From the Iconography*, 1630, courtesy of the Metropolitan Museum of Art, New York, NY, bequest of Mary Stillman Harkness, 1950, Accession Number: 50.583.4.

P. 88, Sandro Botticelli, *The Virgin and Child*, c. 1490, courtesy of Harvard Art Museums/Fogg Museum, Cambridge, MA, bequest of Grenville L. Winthrop, 1943.105, photo: Imaging Department © President and Fellows of Harvard College.

P. 90, Ellsworth Kelly, *Untitled*, c. 1964, courtesy of Harvard Art Museums/Fogg Museum, Cambridge, MA, gift of Mrs. Susan Morse Hilles, transferred from Student Print Rental, M26230, photo: Imaging Department © President and Fellows of Harvard College.

P. 92, Daniel Thomas Moran, *Samuel Menashe*, c. 2004 courtesy of the photographer.

P. 94, Joseph Marioni, *Yellow Painting*, 1999, courtesy of Harvard Art Museums/ Fogg Museum, Cambridge, MA, purchase through the generosity of Dr. Irving and Natalie Forman in honor of Michael Fried, 2000.241, copyright: © Joseph Marioni, photo: Imaging Department © President and Fellows of Harvard College.

P. 96, Andy Warhol, *BMW Art Car*, 1979, courtesy of BMW.

P. 96, Ken Done, *BMW Art Car, 1989*, courtesy of BMW.

P. 98, Auguste Rodin, *Dance Movement I*, 1911, courtesy of Harvard Art Museums/Fogg Museum, Cambridge, MA, William M. Prichard and Louise Haskell Daly Funds, 1966.88, photo: Imaging Department © President and Fellows of Harvard College.

P. 98, Camille Claudel, *The Implorer*, 1898 and c. 1905, courtesy of the Metropolitan Museum of Art, New York, NY, gift of Iris and B. Gerald Cantor, 1990, Accession Number: 1990.171.

P. 98, Mary Cassatt, *Portrait of the Artist*, 1878, courtesy of the Metropolitan Museum of Art, New York, NY, bequest of Edith H. Proskauer, 1975, Accession Number: 1975.319.1.

P. 100, Christo & Jeanne-Claude, *The Gates*, 2005, photo by Morris Pearl.

P. 100, Susan Israel, *Rising Tides*, public art at Courthouse T Station, Boston, Massachusetts, 2014, courtesy of the artist.

P. 102, Greg Stone, *True Colors*, 2015, courtesy of the "artist."

P. 104, *Blind Spot Assist Ad*, courtesy of Mercedes-Benz.

P. 106, Vincent van Gogh, *Green Wheat Fields*, Auvers, 1890, courtesy of the National Gallery of Art, Washington, D.C., Collection of Mr. and Mrs. Paul Mellon, Accession Number: 2013.122.1.

P. 108, *Thomapyrin Paradox Ad*, courtesy of Boehringer Ingelheim. Ad agency: Euro RSCG Duesseldorf, Germany.

P. 110, *Ernest Hemingway* during a shooting party organized by John Meyer, 1940 - 1941. Sun Valley, ID, Robert Capa © International Center of Photography.

P. 112, Frank Gehry and Vlado Milunić, *Dancing House*, 1992 – 1996, photo by Dino Quinzani.

ABOUT THE AUTHOR

Greg Stone, president of Stone Communications, is a media strategist and independent producer in the Boston area. Before founding his company, he was a writer at Time Inc. in New York and a TV reporter in Minneapolis, Boston, and on PBS. He blogs regularly for the *Huffington Post* and has published in the *Harvard Business Review* and the academic journal *Philosophy and Literature*. This book is based on decades of creative endeavors.

Greg graduated with honors from Harvard College and earned master's degrees from Columbia University in journalism and business. Visit gregstone.com for more details.